Bonnie Melton
November, 2020

MOOD INDIGO

D0166170

MOOD INDIGO

Jeanne Heuving

selva oscura press • chicago, illinois

Published by selva oscura press
selvaoscurapress.com

© 2019 by Jeanne Heuving
All rights reserved
Printed in the United States of America

First Edition

ISBN: 978-0-9909453-4-5

Thank you for complying with copyright laws and for not reproducing or distributing
this book in any form or by any means without permission from the publisher.

Design and typesetting by Margaret Tedesco
Text set in Optima
Printing: McNaughton & Gunn

Cover image: Tam Joseph, *Under the Sea Under the Sea*, early 1990s.
Mixed media, pastel, photography, and photo-copied texts on hand-
constructed paper, 200 x 150 cm. Texts from Chinua Achebe,
Ayi Kwei Armah, and Malcolm X, among others. Courtesy of the artist.

Distributed by Small Press Distribution
1341 Seventh Street, Berkeley, CA 94710
www.spdbooks.org

a 501c3 nonprofit

in memory of Kathleen Fraser (1935–2019)

The form of prose is the accuracy of its subject matter—how best to expose the multiform phases of its material.

The form of poetry is related to the movements of the imagination revealed in words—or whatever it may be—

—William Carlos Williams

The player advances to the area, an unknown totality, made whole thru self-analysis (improvisation), the conscious manipulation of known material.

—Cecil Taylor

1.

To begin with ink. I scratch my paper with pen, making abrasions, little torn pieces of pulp, ink soaking into the fibers. My hand moves down the page, ink marking its passage, seeming ahead and behind it. Inks are low lying grasslands subject to flooding by tides. As the salt water rises and seeps into the grass and then quickly covers the depressed land, it makes inky pools of green, combed in one direction with few entanglements. Almost a true level between land and high tide makes for a rich sea marsh, lower by a foot or so, nothing but ink grass growing on it. Some of the sunsets, especially behind the inks, are as fine as you can see anywhere. Indico is

a dye extracted from a plant by the same name but also can be got from woad. The

darkest shade, a kind of blue-black, derived from the indico plant, is the most

valuable. Gathered into bundles of stalks, leaves, and flowers, it is mashed in an

alkinated vat, submerged underwater for several days, the dross then raked out, and

the sediment, the sought after dye, not to be disturbed in the further ladling off of the

liquid. Another technique is to make balls of the gathered wood, stems, and seeds and let dry, then macerate into a pulp and mix with water affixed with ash lye or other alkaline additive. Or remove only the seeds, wait until the seed pods turn black and begin to open on their own, or at least rattle and then submerge. A ship freighted with indico, cochineal and other rich stuff travelling from India and Africa and then onto Europe and North America. On their voyage out, they encountered a sluggish water, black as ink, the depth was so extreme.

2.

To begin with paper. I dye the paper with a thin line of scrawling blue-black. The paper wicks the ink. It is no more than what could be said on paper. I do not wish to paper over it. Paper is made by pressing together moist fibers of cellulose pulp derived from wood, rags or grasses. What makes it paper and not papyrus, from which the word is derived, is that the pulp fibers are macerated and then realigned. Papyrus is made from the lamination of plant life, from the sedgie reed called papyrus, without further decomposition. The outer rind is removed and the sticky fibrous inner pith is cut lengthwise and laid in overlapping strips, to which another layer, at cross angles, is put. While still moist the two layers are hammered together, making them into a single sheet. As far as the eye can see are an abundance of lagoons and water courses fringed with papyrus. To dye is to impregnate tissue and fiber with colour. The number of dippings and the strength and freshness of the indigo determines the intensity of the resulting colour. One of the cottons put into the indigo vat is so thin that it tears like paper and so requires special handling. The dyed cloth is removed to dry and oxidize for twenty-four hours without rinsing. In keeping a stock pot of indigo going in the workroom, it can be reactivated with fructose or other organic materials. If sediment is disturbed allow it to settle. She noticed how the rivers were a-wave with smooth paper reeds and contemplated changing her oaten reed for an oboe.

3.

To begin with cloth. I clothe my body with cloth which holds close to my body. I clothe cloths to protect them from moths. The earliest known uses of cloth were not as a material, but as a thing to wrap or wind about the body. From this winding cloth, we, on the one hand, pass to clothes as garments and, on the other hand, to material, of which all such articles are made. Whole cloth is to be distinguished from a piece cut off for a garment or other item. Whole cloth may be a statement or report that is wholly made up. A characteristic of cloth is how readily its appearance and that of its constitutent fibers can evoke ideas of connectedness and tying. Cloth is soft and pliable and is more likely to fold than to stand up in peaks. Once cloth has been dyed and dried, it is customary to beat the fabric repeatedly with wooden beaters, which both impress the fabric and impart a thin sheen. In some cases additional indigo paste is beaten into the cloth. When it is worn at this stage it rubs off on the skin of the wearer, tinging torso, arms and face with a blue patina. Staring out from her blued body, it was as if the entire world was a blue weft. To dye in the wool, especially when one is a child, is to effect a more thorough and lasting coloration. We must like the scry keep the good seed and cast away the darnell. The conditions under which the scrier can scry are as yet uncertain. I heard the shadows scrying and gave them your name.

4.

To begin with literal. I wish to shore my writing within the littoral. The littoral is the shore between low and high tide or the bog of a river or lake. Rushes abound in the littoral, characterized by their stiff, pithy or hollow stalks. They have joints in the stem and grow in woody places. Because of the constant erosion of tides, trees are felled in the newly forming littoral. Some trees, their roots weakened, are chopped down. The tides with their salty residue blacken the bracken and a host of stumps. A pine tree ablaze, its needles a pool of glistening, is razored by a buzz saw. It hits the mud in a storm of sunlight and sawdust, sap oozing at the cut. The tug of the moon powers the tidal mixing of saltwater and freshwater in an alchemical exchange. Because freshwater is less dense than saltwater, more water flows out into the sea than backward into the watershed. As tidal currents flow past points of land, the water eddies along the lee point. Littoral drift is the sediment moved by the current onto sandy beaches. Oblique winds generate a current parallel to the coast, sending sediment in a swash that then reverses in a backswash. The masthead caught the shrill salt, and sheered the gale. The figurehead had been cut from a block of ship-wood and riveted to the bow. What did she know of the hill and hollow, the sea road? For fine printing, it is needful to shear the nap of the cloth instead of singeing it. I am burned to the quick, but trace rivulets in the shape of little hearts with my fingertip.

5.

To begin with word. Woad as the word for the plant and blue dye produced from it. The word woad is of non-Indo-European origin. Its phonological variety results from the borrowing of this word at different times and places. The technology of dyeing with woad is thought to have spread from the Caucasus and Central Asia into Europe. When Portuguese ships discovered a sea road to India, woad gradually lost out to indigo since it produced a superior color. Having multiple erect stems, arising from a bank of rosette leaves and clusters of tiny yellow leaves, woad is activated by adding an alkaline substance to its leaves, and sometimes seeds. Woading a cloth is done preparatory to making it black. Whenever a dyed cloth is rejected on the ground that it is not properly woaded, it is impossible to remedy it. A piece is sent to the dyer with strict injunctions that it must be woaded, that it must have a ground of blue put into it in order to make the colour of the wool durable. The woadmen harvested and worked the plant until their hands and arms were stained blue-black, woady streaks etching their faces. They stood with a bulging sack of woad balls between them. The sea ore, or woad, as some call it, are the very weeds growing underwater, strewn upon the shore and gathered as fertilizer. Amidst kelp beds, the blue waters appear as inky pools, shifting in coloration with the moving currents. I cast words like sea-woad upon the shore. With so many words, they are as sea-woad, each possessing a distinct coloration. In some areas, woad is treated as a noxious weed and its planting is forbidden. Its seedling is delicate but its spread along muddy shorelines is profuse.

6.

To begin with lake. I make a lake of ink, a reservoir. I hear the lake water lapping with low sounds. A lake is water entirely surrounded by land, and also the basin created by descending streams, however evaporated or non-existent any actual water. The lakish backwater swollen with rain cascades over the escarpment and into the lake below. Nothing can exceed the beauty of the landscape which this lake affords. Torrents of mist rush into the field turning it into a white lake. The precipitate of a particular metal or dye is called a lake. It is washed and laked with water. Instead of blue, I might choose vermillion, carmine or lac. Carmine is a lake of cochineal, derived from the blood of insects. The cochineal is small, rugose, and of a deep mulberry color. It feeds on the moisture and nutrients of cacti and early on was thought to be a berry, only later discovered to be an animal. Cochineal are processed by immersion in hot water and exposure to sunlight, steam, or an oven and then pulverized into carmine. The dye sets more firmly on woolen garments and other protein-based animal fibres such as silk than plant-based material, such as, cotton. Mordant is a substance, typically an inorganic oxide, that combines with a dye or stain and thereby fixes it. I forded several plashes where flourished lascivious shrubs. Hee on Eve began to cast lascivious Eyes. The Fauns and Satyrs, a lascivious race, shrieked at the sight. Their garments are lascivious for being open at the neck and plunging nearly to their waistlines. It should be read in the evening when a breeze passes over the lake. I take the lake of several flowers.

7.

To begin with otter. I otter write about the river otters I have seen, a whole raft of them, slithering above and beneath the water, oily and reptilian. They quilt the sea in regularly spaced parabolic upswellings converging in peaks and ripples. River otters swim in fresh, brackish or salt water, and travel overland for miles, walking, running or bounding. When bounding, the front and hind feet are brought toward each other causing the back to arch and the tail to be lifted off the ground. Otters make trails along the edges of lakes, streams, and other waterways, sometimes leaving little tractor tracks, other times all signs of them disappeared in the convulsing mud. Some river otters take up residence under porches and sheds near the water. Their removal can be treacherous, especially when brooding, since when disturbed they attack humans and other animals. A quilt is a multi-layered textile, distinguished by its tufted construction, and composed of three layers of fiber stitched together, a top cloth, a back cloth, and wadding. When a single piece of fabric is used for the top cloth, quilting is achieved by the threading pattern alone, creating a kind of quilt referred to as a whole cloth. Decorative threads can be sewn through the layers creating knots of two or more threads that make their own grid. African American quilting drew on textile traditions from four civilizations of Central and West Africa. The use of strips reminiscent of lengths of reed and papyrus were interleaved with less regular shapes. Many different cloths and patterns make the best quilts. It takes all kinds of pieces to piece a quilt. Every time there is a break in the pattern, it is a rebirth in the ancestral power of the creator.

8.

To begin with shore. I shore the nap of the fabric. The shore zone is the zone affected by wave action. When the water does not ebb or flow, there is no shore. Walking down the beach, I listen for the back-tracking of the waves rummaging rocks and pebbles. I peer into a tide pool, the many-colored stones are magnified, their irregular indentations grayish in the barely moving waters. I shear a passage close to the water line, my sneakers getting wet. I can hardly shear my way through the heaps of kelp along the beach, maimed or disaffected octopuses. She eats shore grass as an ox, putting her mouth to the ground, to shear and swallow it. To be sheared from myself as in a sexual cut. Discourse in a therapeutic session is worthwhile insofar as it stumbles on itself, or interrupts ongoing thoughts, shearing empty speech. The cut in the signifying chain verifies its unreality because of the subject's arbitrary imposition in it. The syncopation comes down like a blade, a broken claim to connection. The image I get is one of a rickety bridge (sometimes a rickety boat). I drifted off to where it seemed I was being towed into an abandoned harbor. I wasn't exactly a boat but I felt my anchorlessness as a lack, as an inured, eventually visible pit up from which I floated, looking down on what debris looking into it left. Shore ice is the first to freeze at the start of winter and the last to go in the spring. Further down the shore, long pendant shore-grass created a turf of stringy green, higher up sand dunes covered with strand-grass marshalled the cliff. It was heart rending, heart rendering.

9.

To begin with quilt. I take out my box of material and sort through the pieces. I piece and then I quilt. I have never been so knit together than in this quilting of land and sea, cloth and dye. A patchwork of quilted fields and waterways stretches all the way to the sea. Low sun rays glancing off the waters shear the thatched pathway where many feet have trod. I like to do quilts of strings and patches because I can use little and big pieces. When you cut little pieces you've got to study how to put them together and you want to hit it just right. You could begin by making a block and then put it in the center or off to one side, changing the design as you go. I border one strip with another, one color with another, to bring everything out. The colors should shine or burn and the color of one piece should lift up the one next to it. If you know what to make of it and make a change of it, there's something good in it. I put different pieces in there to make it show up, what it is. I hardly ever buy material. That's not what quilting is all about. In order to have thread for piecing and quilting, we unravel flour and meal sacks, and roll it into tight balls. We sew sacks together to make quilt backs and sometimes use them as batting. She is piecing because she carries no thread of connection, no continuity of repair. She sears the rough fibers so that the warmth of her existence, will not seep out of her soft underskin. One should generally avoid padding, but in quilting padding is required. The wadding expands when aerated as do the billows of an accordion. My body quilts into tufts and peaks, pleats and waves. I quilted my lover when he was no longer my friend.

10.

To begin with indigo. I blue my fingers, hands, and face with indigo. I place my fingers over my eyes in a blue weft of seeing. For dying cloth, two things are required of the dye. It has to be absorbed by the material in question, and it has to be absolutely fast. To collect the seeds of the wild blue indigo, wait until the seed pods turn black and begin to open on their own, or at least rattle when shaken. At this point, remove the pods from their stalks and open them fully. The sea has inspired artists for years finding in its blue-black depths an interchanging life and death, and in its crystalline surface an enhanced seeing that magnifies and stills. For a deep and sad blue, as in floating brown kelp beds, mingle Indico and pink. At sunset, view the inks from the hardened crust of sand above this lake of grass and watch as the sinking sun turns the grassy waters ever darker. Adire is a name given to a number of resist dye techniques in which raffia is used. In adire alabere the raffia spine is stripped and sewn in many little stitches into the fabric. In adire oniko small portions of fabric can be pulled into peaks and then tied with raffia, or a portion of the cloth can be wrapped over a seed or rock before being tied. The cloth must be dried before removing the raffia. All my life through, I've been so black and blue. They laugh at you, and scorn you too. What did I do to be so black and blue? Cold empty bed, springs hard as lead. Feel like Old Ned. Wish I was dead. Even the mouse ran from my house.

11.

To begin with indigo. I repeatedly dip cloth into the indigo vat so that with each immersion a small quantity of dye attaches to the fibres and the blue particles accrete. The technical superiority of indigo rests on the fact that it will dye both vegetable and animal fibres and does so with results that cannot be achieved even approximately using any other vegetable dye. An indigo-bath is almost a living creature and reacts swiftly and implacably to any disruption that may occur during the dyeing process, a fact that makes considerable demands on those in charge of it;

calling in no small degree for the ability to watch over the dye. Visible on the surface

of the bath is the bloom, the blue-violet bubbles. Indigo has something of the

complexity of a gothic cathedral, and is very vulnerable. Damage to just one part can

have dire consequences for the whole. Especially after repeated dipping or

immersion of material that is porous and thus harbours a lot of air, the strain on the

solution is considerable. Soon one will see the characteristic signs of the bath

reaching the point of 'dying,' as it used to be called. Its limpidity diminishes and it becomes blueish and cloudy, as the chemicals in it are oxidized and the indigo dye-stuff precipitates. In early days dyers had to rely mostly on the signals from their own senses when judging the condition of the bath during dyeing. You ain't never been blue, no, no, no til you've had that mood indigo. And in the evening when the lights are low I'm so lonely I could cry. When I get that mood indigo I could lay me down and die. That feeling goes stealing right down to my shoes.

12.

To begin with dye. I clutch my pen until a callous forms on my third finger and ink from the over-pressed plastic soaks into my skin. I go to the acquarium to observe the ink-fish as they jet their inky fluids into the water. The dark ink secreted by cephalopods, also called cuttle-fish, is stored in a sac or a bladder, from which it is ejected at will. Ink is a complex medium, composed of solvents, pigments, dyes, resins, lubricants, surfactants, particulate matter, and other materials. Dye-based inks are generally much stronger than pigment-based inks and can produce much more color of a given density per unit of mass. But because dyes are dissolved in the liquid phase, they have a tendency to soak into paper, making the ink less efficient and potentially allowing it to bleed. Each species of cephalopods produces a slightly different coloured ink. A release, with less mucous, simply clouds the water and allows the animal to escape. Another release, with more mucous, meant to fool predators, causes the predator to attack these false bodies, with the cuttlefish then free to swim a great distance without detection. The Greek name for cuttlefish, sepia, is the color of Roman sepia, the color of the dye extracted from a dead cephalopod,

when it contains no mucous. The dark color is obtained from its main constituent,

melanin. She does not know her beauty. She thinks her brown body has no glory. If

she could dance naked under palm trees. And see her image in the river she would

know. But there are no palm trees in the street. And dishwater gives back no image.

13.

To begin with invagination. Dye exists in a reservoir and then traverses the fabric.
An initial bounded material, which is commonly called the beginning, forms
a pocket inside the corpus. The beginning is interminable as ink bleeds through the
piece while cauterizing any simple intent. As the ink fish release false bodies,
pseudomorphs form at roughly the same volume and appearance as the cuttlefish
that emit them. Siphoning water into their mantle, they mix it with the melanin of
their ink sac and prepare for escape. Expanding and then collapsing their mantle,

they jet away with the distillation of ink staying behind as in a pointilest painting, the black bits having the capacity to poison and numb the nerves of advancing predators. Inflated, the large head and eyes and the tentacles of the cephalopod can be discerned, but deflated it is as a scud of folded flesh. Nobody who has not tasted the great cuttlefish, his feelers cut up and stewed in the black ink or sepia which serves him apparently for blood, can imagine how good he is. She cuttles the cloth, laying it in plates, folding and then doubling it back until the entire material lies in piles, the end of the cloth wrapped around to make an envelope or sac. She runs her hands over the cloth because she carries in herself no means of sheathing, no means of enclosing herself, no continuity of repair. She became a quilt maker so that the warmth would not seep out of the soft inner skin of her existence.

14.

To begin with sea road. I travel the sea road between blue waters curving at the horizon and patches of green and yellow fields. I drive the sea road over sand covered asphalt and onto a wet beach crossed with tire marks. The Portuguese discovery of the Sea Road to India around the Cape of Good Hope at the end of the fifteenth century greatly increased the import of indigo to Europe. Indigo dye and cloth from West Africa where Portuguese ships stopped to and from their way around the Cape entered into the trade. With the Sea Road and other sea roads that ensued, indigo that had hitherto been brought to Europe on an overland route and was the color of royalty and aristocracy became much more common. In England and France where woad had been a significant industry, taxation offices in cahoots with dyers created embargoes that made the possession of indigo a crime. Indigo which had to be grown in a tropical climate was vilified as a newly invented, harmful, devouring, and pernicious weed that was the food of the devil. Yet, the corrosive indigo won out as its superior absorption, fastness and color penetrated the quagmire of prohibitions and restrictions. Indigo is superior to all other natural dyes because it can dye any fabric, including cotton and wool. Indigo does not need a mordant as do most other natural dyes, since indigo does not penetrate the fibre but accretes. Early dyers often began with woad and indigo in order to hold fast other colors because they thought these blues acted as a mordant when in fact other dyes simply bonded with them. Practical application is the only mordant which will set things in motion and in memory.

15.

To begin with sea road. In the sixteenth and seventeen centuries the number of sea
roads greatly increased. On both sides of the Atlantic, Africans lived in an ocean of
blue. The everyday throng was a blue sea of indigo. Even the reddish brown earth
was dyed blue where the dyers worked, for everywhere was dripping cloth hung up
to dry. The plantation site was well known for its foul smell and unsanitary
conditions. After the indigo were steeped and the liquids drained away, plants were
no longer needed. These soggy stems were then just dumped creating the conditions

for disease. The smell was so powerful that working around it was miserable. Enslaved Africans who arrived with knowledge of indigo production could be sold at market for many times more than Africans without these capabilities. So esteemed and valuable were knowledgeable indigo workers that a plantation owner specified in his will that Billy shall not be put to any field work, but be kept jobbing on the plantation until indigo season and then shall only work around the vats. Both the European and the African would find themselves influenced by the culture and presence of the other. But the Middle Passage was a death canal for one and not the other. The costs of enslavement would have been driven down exponentially had Europeans taken White slaves directly to America rather than sailing from Europe to Africa to enslave Blacks for American commerce. But what Whites would have gained in economic value, they would have lost in symbolic value, and it is the latter which structures the libidinal economy of civil society.

16.

To begin with blue-black. I watch the blue-black runnels criss-cross the swelling waters moving ever faster and spilling on the shore. It is the form of the wave and not the actual water that travels. She would follow a sea road until her mood changed for the better or precipitated into an anger that would cause her to take the action she had long delayed. In inking her displeasure, it formed etches and creases that could not be erased. Inks grass are not to be confused with sea or ore woad as some call it which is the very weeds growing in the sea upon rocks and stones. Woading a cloth was done preparatory to dyeing it black. Some variation could be seen in the dye job with the creases being a shade darker than rest of the cloth. Every time they play there is something new swinging into the music to make it "hot" and interesting. Then when you listen to a swing band you will begin to recognize that all through the playing of the piece individual instruments will be heard to stand out and then retreat and you will catch new notes and broken-up rhythms you are not at all familiar with. You may have known the melody very well but you will never have heard it played just that way before and will never hear it played just that way again. There is a persistent ethic of variation in musical improvisation; no note is played automatically and even the most inconsequential motif is shaped, and any repetition is varied. The swing is likely to make you feel keen—waiting on edge for the hot variations you feel are coming up at any moment. That is because you recognize, maybe without knowing it, that something really creative is happening right before you. I'm so forlorn. Life's just a thorn.

17.

To begin with mood indigo. My impulse is to convey a mood and not to impart specific grievances causing that mood. A mood can consume the populace as dye penetrates a cloth, altering dispositions that before had seemed inclined to go along with things. Standing on a crust of sand above the inks, a vestige of green could be seen in the dark waters. In a very low tide, the inks are all mud and stranded grass, but when the waters come back in they resume their heft. For a deep and sad Greene, as in the inmost leaves of Trees, mingle Indico and Pink. Common or Flanders blacks are really ultra blue-blacks and purples. True or Spanish black can only be made with copperas mixed with galls, and, optionally steel filings or slip also. When I use the word black I mean in the American sense where anyone who has any colored blood at all, no matter how white, speaks of herself as black. Adjoining White Town stands a much larger Black Town, where Portuguese, Armenians and a great variety of other People live. He had shown how those mood-poems which surge through men can be written down in music as symphonies. There is one fundamental difference between swing and classical music. In classical music, the composer and conductor are all important. The score must be interpreted according to the teachings and traditions of the masters. But in swing the musician—the instrumentalist—is all-important. He must add something to the original composition and do it spontaneously without preparation. Things harder to talk about are the satisfaction of playing because it's the thing you'd rather do than anything else. You ain't never been blue. No, no, no.

18.

To begin with images. I see lines with quarter notes, half notes, full notes, black notes with flags and white notes with dots. I see lines of verse that are as a black and white sea; crests, troughs, strikes, curves. As far as the eye could see were a great abundance of lagoons and water courses fringed with papyrus and palms. The palm fronds lifted and fell as if breathing and the stalks of papyrus moved slightly. Many grasses relish the moist, sticky conditions that a swamp provides. Among the most spectacular are the Caperus Papyrus, the Egyptian paper reed. Sedgie reeds, formerly called papyri, of which paper was made, were replaced by cottons and linens, and eventually wood pulp. I see the line, the end of the line. See Line Woman dressed in green, wears silk stockings with golden seams. Sea Lion Woman dressed in brown, watch out fellows she's gonna get down. Sea Lying Woman, black dress on, for a thousand dollars, she will wail and moan. Each tune, no matter how many times I do it, is different. I trust that instinct that lets me go where I go with the tune. If you're striking at the heart of five thousand people, there's more being plugged into you. There's more electricity coming from you because you're getting it from them and they're getting it from you. It's like when lightning strikes a town, or a hurricane or a tornado. It becomes stronger as it goes through the oceans and the waves get bigger—it gets stronger all the time, because it's been building wave by wave by wave. If she could dance naked under palm trees and see her image in the river she would know. Yes, she would know.

19.

To begin with synthesis. I stand amidst syntheses as a tree in a muddy swamp. The making of objects distinct belongs to synthesis, the making of concepts distinct to analysis. To remember that what in the infant is an elaborate synthesis afterwards becomes in the child and then the adult an instantaneous cognition. He wore a dainty and effeminate pied garment called Synthesis. At feast great persons were wont to change their ordinary clothes for a white Synthesis. Nero was dressed in a loose Synthesis, a dress of white twill, unconfined by any girdle. In reblending the constituent colors, by way of synthesis, we reconstitute white light. Since synthetic indigo was created as Indigo Pure, some uncertainty has existed regarding its tinctorial value as compared with the natural dyestuff. Some think that the impurities in natural indigo add to the richness of its color. To get dyers to use Indigo Pure some of the unpleasant odors of natural indigo were added to the mix to increase its verity and authenticity. Denim was first dyed with natural indigo and then with synthetic indigo. Its look is achieved by the indigo thread passing over two white woofs, such that the outer cloth appears bluish and the inner cloth whitish. The wear of jeans in the areas of most stress creates the faded look and torn threads that some regard as fashionable. Nobel Prize winning chemist Heinrich Caro, head of research at the Badische Anlin Soda Fabrik, figured out the basic chemical structure of indigo by 1846. However it was not until 1897 that the company at last succeeded in launching Indigo Pure onto the market, having spent eighteen million gold marks on research, more than the capital value of the company at the time.

20.

To begin with synchresis. I do not seek refuge in a synthesized pain laced with the small pleasure of succumbing, but turn to synchresis. In synchresis the elements are not synthesized but altered in their make-up into a new thing. Since every word obtains its meaning through synchresis of disparate schema, words end up acquiring a reality of their own. Language has multiple components, each of which has a different biological basis and must be orchestrated in very precise ways in instrumental interventions for students who are at-risk biologically for learning to read. For those with dyslexia, synchresis does not happen or happens in faulty ways, so the best way of correcting for it is to separate out the discrete elements of words that allow for reading to occur—their sound or phonology, their visual look or their orthography and the separation of the parts of speech or morphology. This teaching gives dyslexic brains a jump-start in that it makes every aspect of reading-words explicit. Permanent press is a characteristic of fabric that has been chemically processed to resist wrinkles and hold its shape and involves a series of agents that crosslink cellulose-based fibers. When weak bonds break, wrinkles occur, but an admixture of chemicals create new bonds that act like rungs of a ladder. The stiffened material and the loss of texture turn clothes into tents and casements that do not breathe. In 1893 Charles R. Barnes introduced the term photosyntax in order to denote the chain-like process by which light energy is converted into chemical energy. Photosynthesis soon became the preferred word for referring to the alchemy by which sunlight enables plants to grow.

21.

To begin with synchresis. Synchresis is an acronym formed by telescoping together two words, synchronism and synthesis. Through synchresis, the musician reading a musical score hears musical sounds. Films depend on synchresis as music often drops into the background while forming visuals into something never before seen on land or sea. Homonymy leading to synchresis causes the merging of inflectional categories with the burden of disambiguating meanings shifting to the syntagma. Aphrodisiacs create a synchresis of sex, pleasure, and love into stew-pots that can overwhelm. I bury my nose in the wafting perfumes and only later come up for air. Life only seemed worth living when the threshold between waking and sleeping was worn away by multitudinous images flooding back and forth. Language only seemed itself where sound and image, image and sound interpenetrated with automatic precision and such felicity that no chink was left for the penny-in-the slot called meaning. Kelp gets all of its growth from the photosynthesis of sunlight and sea water nutrients. Giant kelp forests anchored to the ocean floor by hold-fasts, grow toward the sunlight, stipes and blades floating upward and forming mats that shade columns of sea water and the floor below. Gas-filled pods attached to the blades keep the ever expanding canopy afloat. Neither plant nor animal, this wide-ranging algae releases large amounts of oxygen into the air, repairing the earth's atmosphere. Photosynthesis is the process by which almost all of the earth's oxygen is produced and creates more than three times the energy used by all human civilization.

AFTER . . .

I have utilized multiple internet and print sources in order to create the textures of
Mood Indigo, borrowing, riffing, and making. For appropriations that have been
taken from wordings of a singular caste; that is, when an individual's mind and hand
seem indelibly connected to the words engaged, I credit these in "After . . ." . Only
occasionally do I quote verbatim. Often I have fudged or budged a word or two,
and sometimes I have added whole new phrases and sentences, and reordered the
passage. However, all said, I am much beholden to these originators for the following
passages:

2.
Robert Browning, "The rivers were a-wave . . . oboe."

3.
Annette B. Weiner and Jane Schneider, "A characteristic . . . tying."
Laynie Browne, "I heard the shadows . . . name."

4.
H.D., "The masthead . . . the sea road."

6.
John Milton, "Hee . . . Eyes."
William Cowper, "The Fauns . . . sight."

7.
Fu-Kiau Bunseki, "Every time . . . creator."

8.
Jacques Lacan, "To be sheared . . . The cut."
Nathaniel Mackey, "The syncopation . . . left."

9.

Quiltmakers Gee's Bend – Nora Ezell, Joanna Pettway, Sarah Mary Taylor, Lucinda
Toomer, Pecolia Warner, "I like . . . batting."
Anais Nin, "no thread of connection . . . soft underskin."

10.

Fats Waller, Louis Armstrong, Harry Brooks and Andy Razaf, "All my life through . . .
ran from my house."

11.

Gosta Sandberg, "An indigo-bath is almost a living creature . . . during dyeing."
Duke Ellington, Barney Bigard and Irving Mills, "You ain't never . . . shoes."

12.

Nina Simone and William Waring Cuney ,"If she could dance . . . image."

13

Jacques Derrida, "a pocket . . . the corpus."

14.

Jenny Balfour-Paul, "taxation offices . . . devil."

15.

Gosta Sandberg, "On both sides . . . to dry."
Virginia Jelatis, "The smell . . . the vat."
David Eltis and Frank Wilderson, "The costs of . . . civil society."

16.

Fats Waller, Louis Armstrong, Harry Brooks and Andy Razaf, "Every time . . . a thorn."

17.

Zora Neale Hurston, "When I use . . . black."

Duke Ellington, Barney Bigard, and Irving Mills, "There is one . . . No, no, no."

18.

Nina Simone, "Each tune . . . wave."

Nina Simone and William Waring, "If . . . know."

19.

Jenny Balfour-Paul, "Since synthethic. . . at the time."

20.

Elizabeth Aylward and Viriginia Berninger, "Language . . . explicit."

21.

Walter Benjamin, "Life . . . meaning."

Jeanne Heuving is the author of the poetry book *Transducer* (Chax Press) and the cross genre work *Incapacity* (Chiasmus Press), which won a Book of the Year Award from Small Press Traffic in 2004. She recently published *The Transmutation of Love and Avant-Garde Poetics* (Modern and Contemporary Poetics series, University of Alabama Press) and co-edited the collection of essays *Inciting Poetics: Thinking and Writing Poetry* (Recencies Series, University of New Mexico Press). Heuving is a professor in the Interdisciplinary Arts and Science program at the University of Washington (UW) Bothell and is on the graduate faculty in the English Department at UW Seattle. She founded the MFA in Creative Writing & Poetics at UW Bothell and served as its first director. She is the recipient of grants from the Fulbright Foundation, National Endowment for the Humanities, Simpson Humanities Center, and the Beinecke Library at Yale.

ACKNOWLEDGEMENTS

Sections 1-3, *Hambone*, Fall 2019

Other books from selva oscura press:

dog with elizabethan collar by Ken Taylor
Moment's Omen by Nathaniel Mackey
Zippers & Jeans by J. Peter Moore
A Spell in the Pokey: Hugh Walthall Selected Poems Edited by Aldon Lynn Nielsen
*after*Kleist by Matthew Fink
Eroding Witness by Nathaniel Mackey
Veronica: A Suite in X Parts by Erica Hunt

And by Three Count Pour
(an imprint of selva oscura press):

Durham Suite: 5 by Three Count Pour
Anuncio's Last Love Song by Nathaniel Mackey
Southern Colortype by J. Peter Moore
A History of Fire by Dianne Timbin
first the trees, now this by Ken Taylor
[Distressed Properties] by Magdalena Zurawski
Songs In-Between the Day/ Offshore St. Mark by David Need

selvaoscurapress.com